A Letter From The Mountain & Other Poems

Tom Snarsky

Advance Praise for *A Letter From The Mountain & Other Poems*

"Tom Snarsky's *A Letter From The Mountain & Other Poems* reminds me of the deep taproots the trees around me must have to have survived droughts again and again. These are poems whose spirit suggests a deeper life-force exists which could get us through—'it feels impossible, somehow, that you just continue / without knowing what your name means.' Wherever you are in understanding your place in your 'own sense of cause or consequence,' *A Letter From The Mountain & Other Poems* offers an unapologetic clarity I've only ever seen in Tom Snarsky's lines."

—C.T. Salazar,
author of *Headless John the Baptist Hitchhiking*

"At the heart of Tom Snarsky's *A Letter From The Mountain & Other Poems* is the impossible task of surviving the burdensome reality of American capitalism, the speaker continuously offering straight-faced understanding of its hold on our psyche: 'Money is the most boring thing in the world, like breathing / it's annoying when you're forced to think about it // or it feels impossible, somehow, that you just continue / regulating these flows or you die.' But Snarsky flips the idea of what's impossible on its head, the challenge of capitalism's arbitrary grip pitted against the rarer, more beautiful impossibility of a single, un-replicable life. Across these poems, experience a torrential rush of specificity that only this speaker can provide as he meditates on John Ashbery, Tracy Chapman, the recklessness of angels, probiotics, the perfect Mother's Day poem, neural microarchitecture, internet companies, and moonshine. And witness poetry's impossibility, too: the intimacy of a voice extending across the ether, a letter of formal invention that reaches you like '…[a] meadow you hold open // [l]ike a door'."

—Susan L. Leary,
author of *Dressing the Bear*

"We are taxed, indebted, debited, threatened/enticed with bullets, scammed by the internet company and also the internet, imitated by robots, interpolated by information that translates us beyond recognition, transposed from the theory that thinks it has thought of everything to a house nobody can live in-- a house that is only a word.

Tom Snarsky has accumulated with admirable geniality and tact a wealth of living against which the overdrafts of late-stage necro-extractive America still draws its funds.

He practices the long poem as Schuyler and Ashbery did it-- even when he's writing a short poem, the sense of his living prods the silent and deafening theft against which all poetry tilts.

I love his wasps, his albino cockroach-- I even love it when his sick cat farts. He has written a hymn to life, an archive of antidotes to the mind of war and the sin of despair. 'The wedge driven into poetry is poverty,' yet each line earns back in spades what is stolen from us in the bad math of our living. An essential poet."

—Ariana Reines,
author of *The Rose*

A Letter From The Mountain & Other Poems

Tom Snarsky

Copyright © 2025 Tom Snarsky

All Rights Reserved. This book or any portion thereof may not be reproduced, in whole or in part, in any form (beyond that permitted by Sections 107 and 108 of the U.S. Copyright Law and except by reviewers for the public press), without the express written permission of the publisher except for the use of brief quotations in a book review.

Snarsky, Tom / author

A Letter From The Mountain & Other Poems / Tom Snarsky

Poems

ISBN: 979-8-9869524-9-9

Library of Congress Control Number: 2025938724

Edited by: Beth Gordon
Book Design: Amanda McLeod
Cover Art: Norma Cole. Used with permission.
Interior Art: Norma Cole. Used with permission. / MD OMAR FARUK, budi priyanto, Olga Ubirailo, Tanya Syrytsyna, Yuliya Baranych, addillum, AlphaStd, all via iStock.
Cover Design: Amanda McLeod

PUBLISHER
Animal Heart Press
Asheville, NC 28803
www.animalheartpress.net

*for Kristi, who brought me to
the mountain*

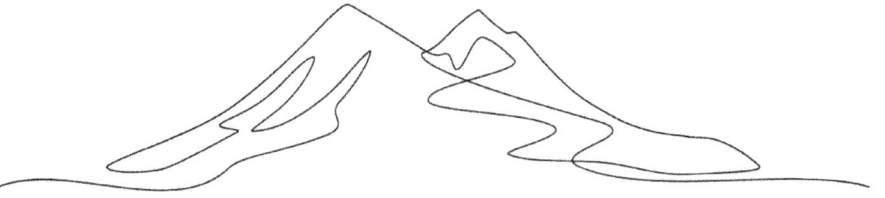

Table of Contents

Sturgeon Moon	1
A Letter From The Mountain	3
Poem	36
Duckweed	37
Orange Rural Fire	38
Sonnet	40
Sonnet	41
Late Fee	42
Prose Poem	43
Pan-American Strawberries	44
15 FLORÉAL	46
Metal, Pennsylvania	47
Upstream Color	51
Low Fidelity	52
OOAK	53
Untitled	54
Idyll for Large Orchestra	57
Tax Crimes Handbook	58
Exactly Fifty Teeth	59
Alcohol, Brutalism, Confetti	60
William Bronk	61
William Blake	62
William Butler Yeats	63
Poem	64
Bag of Water	68

Song	69
Tree of Life	70
Espresso Powder	71
Sheep in the Pyrenees	72
Keep Talking	73
Notes & Acknowledgments	75
About the Author	77

Sturgeon Moon

In the normie yarrow of waking life
my body is an industry

secret, how do you guard
what you don't know, the flowers

trying to get us out of the '80s
safely like REM from *Green*

to *Out of Time*

A Letter From The Mountain

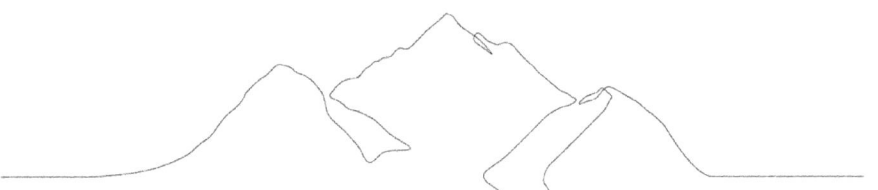

He looked in a glass of the earth and thought he lived in it.

— Wallace Stevens

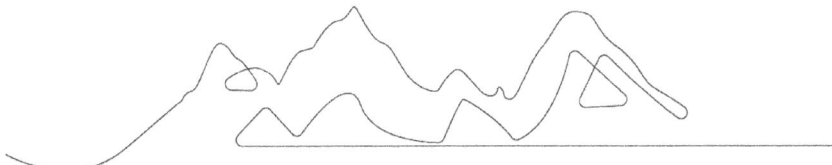

I

My 1st thought was I'd write down every bird
Who came through here without an injury
Or other stated reason not to stop
A winter's feeling sorry for oneself
Flowered into singing by the spring. If
A painter, cloven to ideas instead
Of color, wrote out detailed names for all
Her sketches, you'd probably see that work
As separate from the main thing, canvases
On which a razor taught regret to oil.
As borer bees eventually destroy
The barns or buildings they maneuver thru
En route to copulation or to death
(Or both), I hope you can forgive me for
The wet eyes and shaky hands I brought to
Our life, which would/could've been so much
Easier if I'd made choices or money
Differently. Or more often. Every fall
Has started owing summer time and a
Half for covering September, the pond
Is low & leafless into October
Some years you can still see Halloween koi.
This great American inventor I

Know, he works at the local hardware store
And is surrounded all day by broken
Lamps. It's fifty cents for a really small
Fuse, 5A/120V, though like most
Things you can still get for short money I
Harbor doubt it's all you'll need to fix the
Light you brought in hoping for a miracle.
The painter Agnes Martin was her own
Most difficult critic, cutting painting
After painting up (or having someone
Else cut them up for her) if they didn't
Succeed in expressing innocence (her
Word). Like William Blake karaoke, half
Of how the most of us have deigned to live.
Although, hold on— it's not like I mean to
Say there's anything wrong with that vision,
That hope for one's body of work. I just
Already have this big bouquet of wrongs
I've foisted from the earth and watered well,
A whole entire Harold orchid room
With more rope than any flower could need.
But sun comes. And with it, an improvised
Greeting we should've practiced beforehand
Like our signatures in limited space
Or a play with more than one speaking role.
The gradient of soil from clay to black
At first may seem like not the most thrilling
Spectrum, from reddish brown to the total
Of all colors (or is it pure absence
Of color?), but when it is the difference
Between a fresh-dug pond filling up with
Actual water or not suddenly
It starts to make sense of how people care
About the tiniest variations
Between things, the clarinets entering
A few thousandths of a second later
Becoming synonymous with ruin

Or innovation. The maple tree has
A winged fruit called a samara, which I
Didn't know, but of course once I saw one
Online I knew the fruit behind the name:
A whirlybird (one down, a multitude
To go). Do you think Spinoza ever
Used a lens to look directly into
The sun? Before it was known exactly
What that does to you? I say "before" like
It wasn't known the sun can hurt your eyes,
Clown emoji, but there's something to be
Said for how the ways we know we harm our
Selves've increased manifold, dandelions
By chances strewn and further chances set
In soil rich with N and K and low in
P, with poor decay of organic
Matter. A frog jumps straight into the pond
As I approach. I hear Yahya Hassan:
"Criminals can harbour literary
Qualities," as the frog steals underneath
The ripples. My prolonged study of frogs
Is out of hope I'll learn from them just how
To make a life defined by a surface,
Be unafraid to breathe on either side.
At the very longest last we have reached
The eighty-sixth line, 1986
The year *On the Plurality of Worlds*
Appears, Ashbery's "a winding staircase
with greenish light" perhaps incredulous
Too, I don't know. I always reach for books
When I'm afraid of saying something true.
Like "I will probably not be enough
In the black to cover our local tax
Bills this yr," our household monthly budget
Feels a bit like the flat penny Godspeed
You! Black Emperor included in some
F#A#∞ pressings,

Squashed on a railroad track in Canada
Somewhere (the penny, not the record). I'm
A life insurance proof of concept
Walking around in my tragedy clothes.
It's spring and the grass is already long
Enough to start poking up through the stone
In a few spots, small green Excaliburs.
I think you need to know there is a thing
I think I hope I'm building you toward,
But it's not a sword, or even like one.
A gun's a decent guess for what you hear
A shoebill doing with its beak, with which
It also eats. The Orchid King, Henry
Frederick Conrad Sander, had a son-in-
Law called Henry Moon; they did a big book
Together but it was a terrible
Process because Henry the elder was
A businessman and Henry the younger
Was a "strong-willed artist" (Wikipedia)
Who painted orchids til the day he died
At forty-eight. He framed his work himself,
A European house wren building nest
After blank nest to cradle the future.
Do you think you have already suffered
The worst pain you will know in your life, or
Is it yet to come? What part of the great
Tide of despair are you riding, the ebb
Or the flow? Cattle, naked mole rats laugh
At our fragility. The Amazon
Is at a breaking point, or past it, tweet
#913 of my day
Declares, and in reply I post a poem
By Lyn Hejinian about angels.
The American criterion for
Truth is pragmatism's: a thing is true
If it is useful, if it works. My best
Friend Scott's disability checks from the

Army take forever to get approved
To start arriving, and the first one (with
Back pay) gets sent to an account number
That doesn't exist. They tell him not to
Worry. In a drought summer, the river
Gets low, too rocky to safely canoe.
The first time I said *I love you* to you
Was in French, after not sure how many
Drinks, & my cheeks were on fire w/the word
Love, two Mark Twain tomatoes trespassing
On the Cherokee purple vine my heart
Clung to as it grew out toward you & sky.
It's really hard to talk about that part,
The learning love again post-pain— cliché
Has creeping tendrils, won't let memory
Alone, and healing is so slow that verse
Uniquely fails as vessel for its flow:
You can just listen, or read the next line
Without doubting you'll continue at all.
This fall I'm hoping to have firewood cut
A little bit before the leaves are down—
Not all the wood, nor all the leaves. A start
To make October feel a little less
Like work. Maybe by then I will be less
Worried about money, less overdue
On everything, less constitutional
More situational in my weakness.
By February one debt will be paid
In full— if I forget for a second
How many other ones we have, how the
Interest accrues like plaque or loneliness
I can feel a brief flicker of progress.
The sage is coming in nicely in its
Barrel, furred like the bees who half-visit
On their way to the flowers who don't owe
Anybody anything but color
& sweet scent, pollen which they give freely

Is not debt because it doesn't promise
Any destination, puts nothing in
Writing. The policy at the hardware
Store where the inventor works is you can
Bring in guns so long as the action is
Open and you've kept the ammo separate.
The baby rabbit who lost part of his
Face to a lawnmower is improving,
It's scabbed up and he can drink on his own.
Food is still a dropper situation
But the wildlife rescue people are quote
Cautiously optimistic end of quote.
The other day I learned how, if you drink
Water that's like, manufacturing-pure,
It will start to drink you back— leach salt &
Electrolytes from your saliva, since
The polar water molecules don't have
Anything else around to latch onto.
(It would probably also taste bad, since
Our metric for good-tasting water is
How closely it can match up with our spit.)
They're doing a limited pressing
Of my mom's new record on pink vinyl;
The coastal flooding in Massachusetts
Is on track with a sea level rise of
Two feet by 2050, meaning the
Hurricane barrier in New Bedford
Would need to be closed once or twice/day
To keep pace, which is impossible for
A working port to sustain. Fall River,
Home of Precise Packaging, LLC,
Will be on the receiving end of two
Handheld chemical detection units
So its Fire Department can respond
More quickly to hazardous waste events,
All part of an EPA settlement
Bc Precise Packaging, LLC

Was out of compliance & would've stayed
That way because it's cheaper not to train
The people who handle hazardous waste.
The bottom line sees all trash as just trash.
When we mixed the wallpaper glue ourself
It was laughable how much extra we
Had. I laid it on really thick with the
Insurance people on the phone, tried my
Best to save a few dollars a month but
Still ensure it'd be a cool million
If unexpectedly I pass away.
Earlier this morning I was trying
To remember that line, where I left off,
But I kept thinking "unfortunately"
Instead, a whole prescriptive/descriptive
Scrimmage there, I'm looking for Mother's Day
Poems to post and haven't found one that feels
Right. In another compositional
Update, I finally gave up trying
To make the lines all fit on my phone screen
Without spilling over, which the giant
Two-syllable word "Scrimmage" forced my hand
On, but I think it's better for the poem
Anyway. I don't know what the plastic
Funnel things are called we put at the base
Of the downspouts but it's fun to pick them
Up and hope you might see a snail or toad
Or an albino cockroach like you called
Me over to see once, as it turns out
The white color just meant it had molted
Recently, so maybe later that same
April when I was lying down in the
Barn attic trying to reach those wasp nests
And a bunch of roaches crawled on my legs
Maybe one of them was the same little
Guy, only hardened and darkened by time.
Sometimes being alive feels most like that

Turn-of-the-eighteenth-century French priest
Who spent most of his short life fostering
Devotion to Jesus through Mary. Saint
Louis-Marie Grignion de Montfort
Wrote, *"God the Father made an assemblage*
[O]f all the waters, and He named it the
[S]ea (mare). He has made an assemblage of
[A]ll His graces, and He has called it Ma-
[R]y (Maria)." Marian devotions
Are a great excuse for poetry when
You're sad & young & think that God might know
Your heart's big secret, told in silent pleas
By incognito searches for René
Karl Wilhelm Johann Josef Maria
Or Crevel, who when you learned how he died
It made you cry for days, a silly thing
That became your entire politics.
Speaking of which, here sometimes *you* is you
And sometimes it seems to be me, coward
-Ly, when I don't want to own what I mean.
In the scene from *Personal Shopper* where
Kristen Stewart's character is trying
To explain the sign(s) she hopes to see from
Her brother, her interlocutor asks
If they'd (the sign(s)) be from the afterlife,
To which she replies: "You could call it that;
[Y]ou could call it a million things." Possums
Tend to live for only 1–3 years
In the wild, longer in captivity
But not worlds longer, typical macaws
Can see literal scores of possum life-
Times come and go before wasting disease
Could whisk them away to the rainforest
Or woodland or savannah in the sky.
The oldest one on record lived to be
114; her name was Charlie
But looking into her story online

Pretty quickly devolves into legend,
Like she was Churchill's bird etc.
At least in most versions of the story
She swears vociferously at Hitler,
What Deleuze calls The Powers of the False.
Deleuze's lectures on Leibniz are part
Of what I might be tempted to call the
Many-Storied Edifice of Love™
On one floor of which you can watch
Mother deer shepherd their fawns across roads
Dangerous with rain, one floor down from the
Loop of lava-lamp globs enacting both
Horns of the dialectic dilemma:
The one separating into two and
Two fusing together, becoming one.
Sleep / Restart… / Shut Down… // Lock Screen / Log Out
    Tom…
The bones of my perception are different
Bones than I had running in the forest
As a kid, broke a few, I dream of trees
But never of my cell phone which I've heard
Is common, once when I was pretty young
And Virgin Mobile was still a thing but
I didn't really understand the way
They charged for data I spent $42
Downloading Solitaire at the airport.
In Minesweeper there are impossible
Configurations in that you cannot
Guarantee you'll get them without guessing,
And although now there are no-guess versions
Online that was always part of the thrill
For me, that with total information
You could still be cheek to cheek with raw chance
& not leading. Gertrude Stein: "My idea
[I]s. [/] Yes I know what your idea is." Mold
On the microgreens in the cat litter
Container in the garage on the way

To the landfill, or really the Clarke Co.
Convenience Center open from 10 to
3 on Sundays for an alternative
To liturgy. I bite down on a piece
Of sand and can't eat anymore. The wasp
I killed that had been hovering around
One of the basement fluorescent tube lights
Wasn't a wasp at all, apparently,
But a giant hornet (not the murder
Kind). On the floor, dead, underneath the fridge
It looked a little like a shrimp on ice
Behind the seafood counter, where you go
If you want them still with their legs attached.
It's like there's this mud or something— this thick
Lack of clarity mortaring things, or
Little apiaries shuttering in
Deference to the bears, who are hard to stop
Once they have a scent and a sense of place.
I love when the computer talks to me,
Reminds me that my payment's been declined
Or that a favorite musical artist
Is coming soon to a venue nearby.
Last time in DC the parking was worse
Than the tickets, more evidence against
Cars, though without one idk how I
Would live— twenty minutes from town any
Way you take off the mountain & there are
A lot of ways, good for when the ground is
Wet and the old dead trees start to come down.
If one falls that's too big for a chainsaw
It can lie there Brobdingnagianly
For days, or if you're lucky maybe two
Or more neighbors can come help and between
Multiple saws and a few other tricks
Together you can cut and haul it off.
Today my debts are making me feel sour.
I talk to Jo about the word "is" in

A Noelle Kocot poem and feel better
For a while (♩ *My life…* ♫). I have heard the phrase
It's only money twice in recent days
(Once from a poet, once from a parent)
And both times I felt bad, but for different
Reasons each time. Thinking of another
Job I pass a yellow ROAD NARROWS sign
(Pumpernickel and Mackerel are quiet
In their carrier, probably asleep)
Above a sign that shows my age in miles
Per hour, what I will turn this November.
Mackerel farts and the whole car starts to smell
But I'm grateful, I would have forgotten
To tell the vet how gassy he has been.
We're almost out of all the kinds of food
Again, and I will take any guidance
Re: what to buy to save us from the fumes.
On the way back from the vet I drive by
The first shooting range over the state line;
There's signs just before it and just after,
But the one after is down a hill so
When you crest it for a second you can't
See the name of the range, just a bullet
With YOU JUST PASSED above it in all caps.
It's a probiotic, and a special
Kind of food the vet thinks will do the trick.
There's another supplemental treatment
That would be good but that I can't afford
Right now. Plus I used the wrong credit card
So now all Mackerel's inoculations
Are accruing interest; a financier
With a stake in this rabies medallion.
Gilbert Strang just gave his last linear
Algebra lecture and oddly it was
That, more than all the other signs of time
Passing I am inundated with, that
Got me. The sun and I were in a race

To burn out and I won, but the silver
Medalist, in this case, will draw the crowd.

[this is a placeholder more poem goes here
in fact maybe you could go ahead and
write it, like disaster, like disaster
in a milk-white dress, weddinged at Cana
the invitation is a little false
to set up a spot and step into it
monologue, no foundation on your nose
Pierrot told everyone he could juggle
the moon is at that stage in its cycle
where it's lit as much as a piano
is white keys, Arlequin is less than half
Derain's canvas but most of its color
Pierrot could almost blend into a cloud
Columbine just an idea in this one
safer for American reception
go ask ALICE, luminous mysteries
the tidepool, its biodiversity
middle school science everything you need
remember learning about the sphincters
our planet accreting its piles of trash
both pronouns there helping out w/the lie
who are the people still making music
who surprise and delight you, like maybe
you had thought they'd call it quits years ago
and then suddenly there's this new record
a twelve-inch dark circle in a square sleeve
whose last groove (the record, not the sleeve) locks,
not the emperor's or anybody's
just a quick midnight regret idea
like pizza, tattoos, a Crunchwrap Supreme®
or something less circular, do you know
what you would like your next tattoo to be?
for me it's either *elle n'ignorait pas*
by Anne-Marie Albiach or this line:

But the sad hotels are full (Mark Kirschen)
it's not quite that I don't have any faith
in pictures, there are cartoon possums I
would absolutely put on my body
it's that if I had *elle n'ignorait pas*
on my forearm in the grave there would be
always that one particular question,
n'ignorait what, but the wedge driven in
to poetry is poverty and ink
is expensive so maybe we will wait
a lot of time left til eternity
less til heat death but who, who is counting
the sunsets, who's out there tabulating
the way the year shifts underneath our feet
these lazy ones especially failing
the field sobriety test of meter
in almost every line except this one
and a few select others, Calvin and
Hobbes sledding wordlessly down a steep hill
in one strip from 1987
Calvin's dad says, "NOW HERE'S SOMETHING **YOU**
          CAN
THINK ABOUT. THE AVERAGE COST OF RAISING
A KID TO AGE 18 IS $100,
000. THAT'S A LOT OF MONEY.
[new panel] SO THE QUESTION YOU SHOULD BE
ASKING YOURSELF IS, IS THAT HUNDRED GRAND
A **GIFT**… OR A ***LOAN?***" The little bird's nest
in the curve of the drainpipe's already
empty, the geese who have been spring breaking
by the pond seem to have moved on to some
new fresh water & food source, insects corn
lettuce seed grain grass berry barley leaves
mealworms alfalfa a diversified
Diet of Worms where the birds stand & cannot
do otherwise, testament of late spring]

One of my favorite Norma Cole drawings
Is kind of confusing, figurally—
It could be a bunch of grapes, maybe, or
A big blackberry. There are circles, but
It's like the circles are less important
Than the fact of their relation. Cole's lines
Are accompanied by a newspaper
Clipping— attached probably by glue and
Complicating the whole composition—
that just reads, in full, "Uncertainty dogs"

Slowly doing better at the quiz show
Of your life. "Better the drunken gods of
Greece / Than a life ordained by computers."
— James Laughlin, from "Dawn" (thank you Kim Dorman)
Thursday, feeling like a thug for J. H.
Blair more than usual, pulled a tick off
My leg in the office and felt outside.
Don't Google "How many people in the
US are killed by stray bullets each year"
Or you'll find the Stop Celebratory
Gunfire webpage and wonder how many
Images you'll have to slip into poems
Before this particular écume on
The mass tide of death recedes into the
Royal Farms chicken sandwich billboard of
The soul. From Instagram: "Whom do we want
[T]o pay to imagine our souls for us"
— Ariana Reines. It's easier, right?
Still more emails from the Swedish opera
That put on Lax's *Circus of the Sun*
& gave me a free ticket because I
Couldn't figure out how to buy my own,
Since my debit card doesn't do euros
Or hates international transactions
Or I'm on a list, I don't know. Rimbaud
Is buried in Ardennes, Tracy Chapman

Performs "Talkin' about a Revolution"
From home, Adam & Eve leave the garden,
I read and post a poem about spring snow.

A woman with lung cancer is dying
Not just of the disease, but of the fact
She had to wait until her sixty-fifth
Birthday so she could afford to be di-
Agnosed. Pulpy kidney is a common
Infection in young lambs feeding on lush
Pasture; while they're rapidly growing, a
Bacterium that should stay in the
Intestines can begin to multiply
Out of control and produce a toxin
Enough of which will kill the animal.
From a random page of today's Houellebecq:
"Peut-être, quelque part, l'avenir vous attend."

If you're a villain, you begin with ten
Chips, but you lose one each day. If you're a
Hero, you get ten days, and each day you
Survive you get a chip. The strategy
With the highest success rate is a mix
Of hero and villain tactics, losing
A little each day, trying to survive.
Krzysztof Komeda's piano playing
On *Astigmatic Live* is a depth charge,
An allegation the rhythm section
Cannot beat. I don't know how to solder
In a replacement thermal protector
For the fan motor, so I guess it'll need
A new fan. That's one of my favorite jokes,
Looks like your X needs a new X, but who's
To say they don't have one already, or
Two, or enough to clog the pushdown stack
Of memory to the point where you don't
Have to do this, you know, continue on

The path of righteousness beset on all
Sides by the tyranny of evil men.
That's not what I meant to say the other
Day when I got snippy with you, my bones
Were full of reasons to need money and
Their rattles & cracks got me panicky,
Made me forget the love letter feeling
In my stupid heat. A daffodil moon
Swims up through our awareness into day,
Decides to stay for most of the morning.
Maybe, somewhere, the future waits for you.

II

Sunday is the foxes' day of rest. It's going to get harder,
no minimum, reckless angels forgetting their power.

III

The two brothers who lived on the mountain
Were moonshiners, & stole each other's still
So many times that local history's
Relieved itself of any fact of an
"Original" owner; where the yeast is
Tickling the proofing parrot, where sugar
Conspires for two rounds of fermentation
Toward the sour fecundity of
Ethanol— that is where "ownership" lies,
If it is to lie anywhere at all,
As the brothers must have done on Christmas
To keep up above-board appearances.
Ownership is a word one says when scared
That the little interferences be-
Tween one's own sense of cause or consequence
& another's will grow to a choppy
Head, but you don't really want to work it
Out, do you, all those pronoun shifts and o-
Verflowing bathtubs. The power strip floats
In a flip flop, I won't be Gummoing
The whole rest of this but please bear with me,
There's a coffee shop ten minutes from where
I live called Bullets and Beans where you can

Buy ammunition and caffeine with the
Same american money. It's getting
Weird here, creepy and wet, room for sorrow
Pricier even as you don't want to
Fill it with anything, or keep a key.
One of my favorite Norma Cole drawings
Is of a tree, or at least that's what I
Could most readily recognize it as.
It manages quite a lot of texture
With only a few (8? 9?) pencil lines.
When Cedric sings "Turn the 8 into a
9" in "The Requisition" I don't know
What he means, but I know what he means when
He sings on "Shore Story" about making
Them nervous on the phone, whoever can
Hear. Jack Spicer reads *The Holy Grail* drunk
& upends my whole life, that line in the
Book of Magazine Verse about the chill
In the speaker's bones that runs almost all
The way through to the right end of the page.
"I am going north looking for the source
[O]f the chill in my bones." It is boring
To write about not being able to
Do or pay things, but it is true, so I
Write it waiting for the dogs to show up.
When they do they will demand a leader
The same way a spring morning demands dew.
I thought the turkey was a peacock and
I even called her by the wrong name and
I don't think either of them would be thrilled
By my misprision. Bye my misprision,
See you in the Pyrenees with the lambs.

IV

Probably the most important factor in determining a person's politics, that I have seen, is the way they relate to ideas of mass psychosis or mass delusion. If they think of it as a *they* or *we* thing, if they think we can be helped.

V

"2039 was the year we learned
[E]nough neural microarchitecture
& implanting to begin serious
[A]ttempts at 'rewiring,' though to call it
[T]hat alone is to miss many of the
[S]ocial and cultural reasons for why
[T]he practice became so widespread. People—
[P]hilosophers, theorists, ethicists, a
[G]ood chunk of the reading public— discussed
[T]he relative merits, rehashed Shelley
&c., but most people agreed
[T]o have it done in that first wave because
[E]conomical advantageousness
[I]s difficult to dispute. Companies
[P]aid for the procedures en masse, called them
Fellowships or similar names that made
[P]arents want them for their children, & that
[W]as that: the first fleet of implantees, once
[Y]ou correct for the deaths, was on record
[A]s the happiest, most productive group
[O]f workers the world had ever seen. They
[D]id their jobs— many of which were really

[H]andmaidenships to AI, like the old
[V]ideo captioners used to do, re-
[S]aying televised lines as slow & clear
[A]s possible to give the transcription
[S]oftware a fighting chance— with aplomb. Then
[T]he second wave, then Consolidation
[A]nd after that is the world we know now,
[P]leasure centers reordained to serve you
[I]nstead of the evolutionary
[I]mperative, so you can wake up each
[D]ay with the same thrill as if it was your
[F]irst day on the job again, everything
[S]till to be discovered, still as novel
& exciting as when you first became
[G]ood at your assigned tasks, when the firings
[I]n your nucleus accumbens give you
[A] sense of pride and accomplishment no
[E]xternal validation need bother
[T]rying to equal." "The HDMI
[C]able as we know it became standard
[I]n part because it includes copyright
[P]rotection in its very hardware, and
HDCP (High-bandwidth Digital
[C]ontent Protection) was strenuously
[L]obbied for by Intel Corp. and others."
"Lots of scary climate change statistics
[B]egin, 'By 2050…' but we've been
[O]ver 400ppm on the
Keeling curve for years, which we last achieved
[A]s a planet during the Pliocene,
[T]he first earthly period with horses."

VI

When you're alone, sitting with the quiet version of your passion, a wreath of ice around your head, the mountain road curving—

What can the lamb say?

VII

The theories think they've thought of everything.
La teorioj opinias ili pensis pri ĉio.
Teooriad arvavad, et nad mõelnud kõike.
Teoryang tingin inisip nila ng lahat.
Teoria luulevat ajatellut kaikkea.
Théorie pense qu'ils ont pensé à tout.
Teoría creo que pensaron en todo.
თეორია ვფიქრობ ფიქრობდა ყველაფერი.
Ich dachte an die Theorie von allem.
Σκέφτηκα της θεωρίας των πάντων.
હું બધું ના સિદ્ધાંત છે.
Mwen gen yon teyori nan tout bagay.
Ina da ka'idar duk abin.
הבל של תאוריה לי יש.
मैं सब कुछ का एक सिद्धांत है.
Kuv muaj ib tug kev tshawb xav ntawm txhua yam.
Van egy elméletem mindent.
Ég hef kenningu um allt.
M nwere Ozizi nke ihe niile.
Saya memiliki semua Guru.
Tá mé go léir ar an Gúrú.
Ho tutto il guru.

私はすべての教祖を持っている。
Aku duwe guru kabeh.
ನಾನು ಎಲ್ಲಾ ಶಿಕ್ಷಕರು ಹೊಂದಿವೆ.
ខ្ញុំមានទាំងអស់នេក្រូ។
나는 교사 다 갖고있다.
ຂ້າພະເຈົ້າມີຄູສອນ.
Doctorem.
Ārsts.
Daktaras.
Доктор.
Doktor.
Doctor.
Doktor.
Doktor.
Doktor.
डाक्टरहरु।
Leger.

گڈ.

Leger.
Leger.
Léger.
Léger.
Леже.
Легер.
Leger.
Leger.
Børnene.
Børnene.
Børnene.
Børnene.
Børnene.
Børnene.
Børnene.
Børnene.
НАРОДИВСЯ додому.

31

Tạo nhà.
Creu cartref.

Tẹlẹ ile.
Ikhaya yangaphambili.
Voormalige huis.
Ish shtëpi.

Նախկին տուն.
Etxe zahar.
Стары дом.
পুরোনো ঘর.
Stara kuća.
Стара къща.
Antiga casa.
Kanhi nga panimalay.
故居。
故居。
Kuća.
Dům.
Hus.
Huis.
House.

گھر ہوتا پیدا.

היים שאָן.

السابق المنزل.

*The mountain
smiles what is
in the mountain*

— David Melnick

*It is Monday, my nudes
are in a training set
for some AI somewhere
a dry lizard dead &
spread out on the stone
if you feed a lizard
too much fat their liver
will eventually give
up trying to process it &
will instead go the
storage route, the trouble
there being after a
while the fatty liver can't
process toxins the
right way so the immune
system weakens
as if the lizard were not
already susceptible
to the eagle's sharp eye*

Poem

The trick is not to care too much
about fidelity. Let the loss
-y quality of the audio become

another element in
the composition, the under
-study's voice quivering a little

for the first two songs. It's been
a long time since seeing a bear on the moun
-tain; once the beekeeper left,

packed his bees up & brought them to
someplace safer (electric light & a neighbor
-hood watch), they did the opposite

of all my loans
& lost interest

Duckweed

I forget to press the moon
button & sleep badly. Design
is like a hurt bird hopping
between little islands
on human forgetfulness's lake.

As a person your first night
touches you & leaves
this impression, to be picked
up later as seasonal
depression or a dark night

of the soul, or just lingering
like set dressing until the grave
error of being alive shows
a smidge too much leg

Orange Rural Fire

This is a treatise on the art
of wanting things you cannot have,
whether it's because someone
else has them & won't give them up
or because schools of fish
are becoming more and more
selective with time, the bigger pools
of applicants winnowing
slowly enough for them to get away
with certain trickeries—
like a jut of metal near the stream
still appearing strong & straight
despite having witnessed
years & years & years of rain,
so an accidental deer-nudge
is enough to break it clean
in two and set the rust flakes loose

to brighten the mud. I end up
doing that a lot, breaking things
that aren't mine— the trick is
to do it like the deer does it,
not on purpose but just because
you were trying to get a drink
that, whether or not you knew
it, would put gross stuff in your blood
and turn you into a problem.
Cherry trees don't grow here
natively, they have to be brought in

& can't be shaded by bigger trees
or buildings. They need deep,
well-draining soil, six hours
of sunlight a day, and if you don't care
if the fruit is sour that's really it

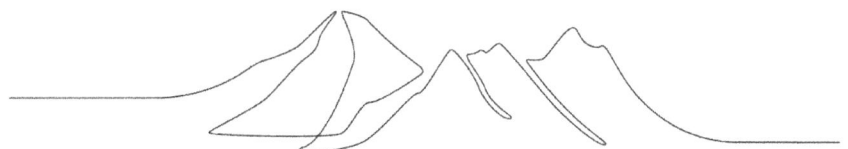

Sonnet

In the dark room a reliable ocean
sounds mix on YouTube replaces day
and night with barely
-perceptible differences in volume
between high and low tide. No birds
ever seem to get near the mic,
which is like a miracle if the kind of miracle
you're into doesn't have birds in it.

In the reliable ocean sounds mix on You
Tube's comments section, there's one guy
with no likes or replies saying "Thank you,
this video helps my son
fall asleep, nothing else has worked as well
as this video."

Sonnet

I wish money was more like a cat than a dog

I bit time & it bent so I knew it was fake

Like wage caps or the full moon Bruce

Almighty pulls down to earth for Jennifer

Aniston's character, whose name is Grace

At this time of writing for $8.99 on Amazon

You can buy a print of this still from the film:

REDACTED*

[Alt text: Bruce holds Grace's shoulders

As they both stare up & left out of frame]

The seller's item description gives a little

warning: *The image you see is true*

to the quality of the photograph, including,

[sic] *coloring.* [sic] *focus and lighting.*

It will not be better than what you see.

Late Fee

It's just me and wild life
trading blows for bantams
in the batting cages. I've

> so little money left
> I'm doing Human Intelligence
> Tasks for fractions

of a penny each, like eating
a few pieces of wet rice
that fell midstride on top

> of a shoe. You think
> I'm ready for the big time,
> Mr. Eland, just wait

until you've seen me
deduplicate data,
transcribe a little video

> a family sitting down
> to dinner together, white
> plates of greens

beneath their silver forks
[heavy breathing]
[inaudible]

Prose Poem

Another day in the ruinous world, eating
peanut butter off a knife.

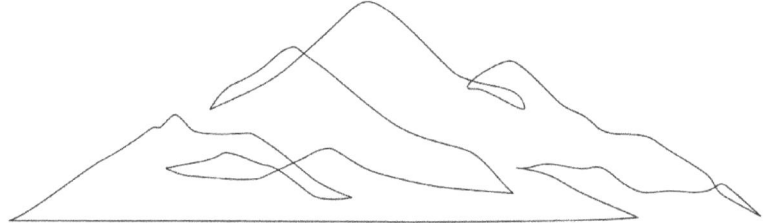

Pan-American Strawberries

Someone I made up
asked me about
the question of form
& constraint in poetry,
like is it better
to write with one ear
bent to certain rules
/traditions or is it
better just to let it all
in, & I was reminded
that sfdt.com
Stick Figure Death
Theater dot com
where you used
to be able to watch
stick figures kill
each other
in increasingly
creative & sophist
icated ways
is now a porn site,
a particularly run
-of-the-mill one
I guess I replied
it isn't so much one
or the other, it's more
when the theme
changes, so
do the variations,

almost as fun
as playing baseball,
but not by much.
Uhra-Beata Simberg
-Ehrström, years
& years after her dad
paints *The Wounded*
Angel, designs a
rya rug *Pathetique*
that when you see it
executed, has
a woven signature,
"USE"

15 FLORÉAL

and really, therapy today
will need to be about going back
to those flybottles of history
when the landlords weren't winning,

Andromache, a vision
of loss so monumental it becomes writ
into a name, becomes etymological
like how when you get stuck writing
a poem you can go back to the dictionary

and divine, pray for the holy food
of sense to be meted out to you
by the birds who have never been landlords
who have resisted anti-bird architecture
however they could

and lost, sometimes, but also
there's a forty-second video called
Bird Throws Anti-Nesting Spikes Off Ledge
that can be like a little liturgy for me

and you, our improvised nest
where we clean the honey jars
and hang up your embroideries,
matching pillows, a bug that says Don't
Bug Me and a snail that says Don't Rush Me

Metal, Pennsylvania

The internet company is fucking us over

& recourse is

another internet company

The two geese

who have been staying

if they have babies it will be bad

for the pond

I am worried about teachers

killing themselves

or being killed

Kristi is a teacher I chickened out

A implies B

if A

there is a sickened knot in me

thinking about all this

heinous shit being gotten away with

at our expense

getting screwed by satellite

so I can send my little

emails

cant slow down your eyes enough

cant match your ear

when you read a prayer too fast or

get ahead of the music

if you feel sick at night at the world

thats normal

the worlds sick at night

the checking accounts bracing

for mornings autopay

like birdshot removed in an autopsy

from the ass of the architect

who built this

a six year old

shot his teacher in Newport News

his mother was indicted

& the world

kept on turning

all of this learnable

even on scam internet

Kristi goes to school every day

the man

in the post office jokes about showing up

to his contractors house

with a .22

its a dumb ragged receipt this

scurrilous breath

wasted

like contraceptives on the waterfowl

like a formal complaint

I am worried about former teachers

killing themselves

writing whole poetry

books about it

clandestinely

musing late

at night about how destiny hides

in that word, clandestinely

like lacustrine, it shines

like clam, it has a secret

a nacre

a valve

a foot

two feet

spondee

I am

withdrawn

like funds

or that one student

you might need

to talk to

for an extra few minutes today

see whats going on

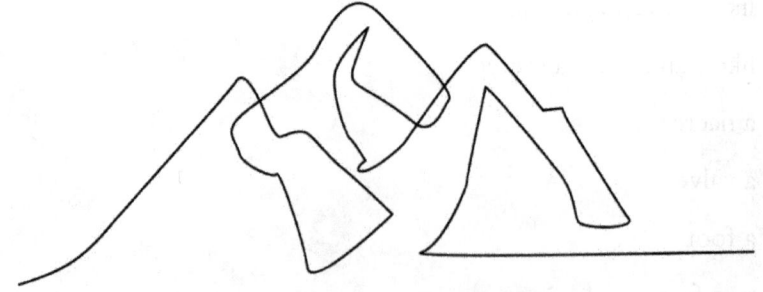

Upstream Color

In the picture the book is angled
so all you can see is *Selected Poems of Rain*

the American forecast continues to be
deli meat & Bud Light violence

I wrote my love a song & pulled out
the vocal track using a free online separator

played the vox for the pigs & the chords
for the chickens over water + feed

to make a good slop try equal parts
fresh & spent barley, + if you have enough

sour milk in there it will go to cheese
in the pot (not in the sense

gambling gives to either of those
words, but in their much acuter sense

of smell), also a possible salve
for the sore day after

your stick-and-poke
tattoo, WWtBdCD, *What*

Would the Baron de Charlus Do,
would it also involve pigs

& being in pain

Low Fidelity

While out ground truthing I found
an animal skull. It had given up
its career selling time to the forest
to tell it on the forest floor instead

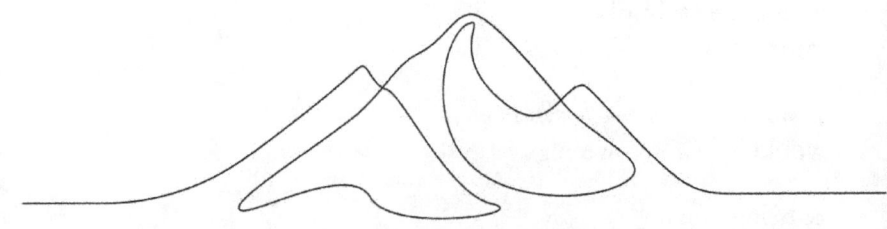

OOAK

The guy doing the executions today
is still learning. When he can't find a vein
people lean in close to him, all in
the learning stance. When he graduates

& his learner's permit is converted
(like pyrite into gold
bullion by the expert alchemist, showing
a student the way) into a license to kill,

when he can finally put away his
training set of mirrors—
the clarinet sonatina plays through
on Side B without a pop or skip

& every body finds its specific gravity,
turns over all the rocks, greets the worms

Untitled

I was making one last serious attempt
at my hands, the palms bruised & caked
with dirt after trying to get well

water up through our overfine filter
which was like the opposite of an hourglass
the way it contained itself & swirled

against gravity. I think the biggest con
is thinking
there's only one big love in one

's life, & like a wave you either catch it
or you don't, & that in the form
er case one should be celebrated

& in the latter pitied or made
tragic, what am I doing I'm *dancing*
like a March idea, like Chopin

for whom dance was one of the languages
like mathematics or love, both flat
tering instances of Polish culture

when you think of our record in war
there is so much anti-trans stuff
on social media right now I am

kind of lost, Alfred Tarski writes
You will not find in semantics any remedy

for decayed teeth or illusions

of grandeur or class conflicts. Nor is
semantics a device for establishing
that everyone except the speaker

and his friends is speaking nonsense.
The deer don't say anything
& the birds, the birds are wrong

loudly. Jack Spicer, who studied
semantics among other
things: *They said he was nineteen;*

he had been kissed [/] So
many times his face was frozen closed
like a topological set or

a Massachusetts liquor store
on Sunday. The aura
is like rock-bottom-of-a-gift-bag

meets ten-flowers-all-dried
-out-because-we-have-no-water
-though-they-probably-would've-taken

-the-dirty-water just fine
Boston you're not home. Jack
at the BPL Rare Book Room

shuffling a series of circumstances
into place that will make
possible *After Lorca* & really all

the books in the *Collected*
Books which doesn't look back
at any of the one-night stands, has

a healthy sense of shame that way

like a shy bullet would rather stay
in its casing than visit the brain

of a hart. I did have one love
& then I had another
& another, rainstorms rolling over

the mountain & through
the river valley, bright fog burning
off for the dew to shine

Idyll for Large Orchestra

Gonna sit
Real quiet
& listen

See if
The truth
Gives up

Its position

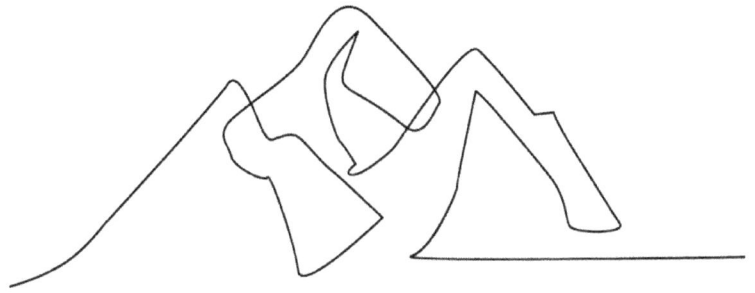

Tax Crimes Handbook

Networking with the fallen angels
In a waiting room at the end of all shame

Telling the same story to the rotorvator
That you told to the sea

Help me
I belong in a whisper cart

Not here
Your fear has a new tenant named Next

Meal the steel mill shut for a day and lost
So much money it had to close

She applied for the job as
A nurse had all the relevant clothes *Help me*

I belong in a whisper cart
Not here

Exactly Fifty Teeth

I sat in the car and let the drama of breathing happen for a minute. It was lenten air, but weightless. *Sorry* hadn't cut my tongue yet when you called so I picked up and let it hang there, an ambient temperature sensor knocked loose in a crash. *Hi* you tried. I thought about my answer, which could've been a far-off bird or nothing. The river was moving & high, like a friend's confession of something you've gone perceptibly grayer having had for years to pretend not to know.

How are you?

There's a blue question underneath most decisions, curled up like a pill bug and still growing legs. I don't think it's violent not to say anything. I don't think it is. The rainbow pattern in your pillow, how it was easier to tell the two purples apart if you'd drooled a little in the night. Clean it was harder to see, more like one thick bruised outer layer protecting the inner bands from the sky. Without it the most like parts would touch.

Alcohol, Brutalism, Confetti

By the dry Potomac my eyes
Were not dry. By the low Shenandoah
I apologized, said garbage like
It's just been a lot lately or
*I don't know why, I just am. It's not
Your fault*, fall coming
Later & later in the year, winter
Shunting itself over
So it never feels like it begins
Anymore in December

I am under the fat wing of god
& it's mostly microphones, here,
for detecting the tiniest sounds
for detecting the tiniest sounds

William Bronk

I always heard it as *god*
is *taking Demerol* on "Morphine"
off *Blood on the Dancefloor*

not *he's* who is he the religious poet
asks what does he want
a school fee or a sacrifice

the dogs or cancer of American
movies will he go
humbly among the people

will he catch their grain
in a shared basket
conscience of the king

an umbrella close enough to the sun
could parry the light of the world

William Blake

& what could the imagination say
of the torturer's horse, that it knew
the meaning of eating? that it threw

crumbs in the path of the king?
the leavening agent, beset
on all sides by traitors

cracks the proverbial bitter pill
& will rise, on the last day.
I pray, as ever, for the shape

of clean water
on which the last two or three
Tyrants have been silent.

do you remember
what the painter said
he'd do if he found the right blue

William Butler Yeats

It all rhymes, sometimes
kind of grossly like
dog slobber in a hot car
parked by a lake.

I no longer live
in a state where you can
get 5¢ for turning
in your uncrushed Cokes

which has diminished my
sense of possibility
& made me want to drive
across state lines

my metal car full of metal

Poem

Money is the most boring thing in the world, like breathing
it's annoying when you're forced to think about it

or it feels impossible, somehow, that you just continue
regulating these flows or you die. I dug up a snail shell

& it was impossible for my naked eye to tell if its inhabitant
    had died
beforehand or if my shovel killed it, if *I* killed it with my
    shovel to be

more precise, I feel a bit American writing this
in the vanishing hours of the Fourth of July, entering the great

U.S.A. tradition of debating whether actions can be attributed
to objects (shovels don't kill snails, people

do), whether corporations can rightly be understood
as people, my LLC was depressed and died by messy suicide
    so

their dependent only gets the money paid directly into
their life insurance policy, nothing like the million dollars

the coverage otherwise would have entitled them to, a little
pasture of capital with a few goats to keep things trim

& in milk. Honey, your body is floating down the river, did
    you want

to attach a mind? Robert Lowell calls Rimbaud's soldier

a "conscript" in his rendition of "Le dormeur du val" and I
 promise
I am not offering you this as some disconnected literary

detail, I think the deux trous rouges have everything to do
with capital's vampire bite and all it sucks out of each of us,

our feet in the gladioli and our hands busy refreshing
the makeup we've applied to the corpses of our lives, dead
 somewhere

between childhood and young-adulthood at the moment
when we had to take debt's bullet in our teeth

& bite down. From that point on it's just uphill bleeding
or it feels impossible, somehow, that you just continue

without knowing what your name means, without responding
appropriately to all correspondence heretofore received,

Thank you so much for your kind message. All the best,
in 2016 the Bethlehem Steel Mill caught fire in (no way)

Lackawanna, New York, all the reports say a fire broke out
but broke *in* feels more right, the air gone anhedonically into
 one big smoke cloud

which has become the norm now, no? I can joke about this
because no one died in the Bethlehem fire, though the one
 person

injured might have some notes, and of course a poet
of a certain race & gender giving himself permission to make

"jokes" is a bit American, too, or at least the getting

away scot-free with it is, I've never paid tax on a joke

but I have on getting paid for a poem & on income from both
    my jobs
("jobs" just a couple small transpositions from "joke,"

it's a theorem you prove somewhere in discrete math
that any permutation can be paraphrased as a composition

of transpositions, in other words we can build up
large derangements out of tiny ones, just switches, really,

like on a philosophy trolley. From these little decisions
all disorder is born). Earlier I demurred from responding in a
    Twitter

thread about what poetry books should do; I almost said
my favorite poetry books are the ones that show

the reader some rough waters, but also carry them through
the building of a (possibly quite provisional) kind of craft

from within which reader & poet alike can survive the roil,
find Fiona Apple's calm atop the surf rather than under

the waves, I don't know, I didn't post it because it felt hokey
or too metaphorical to be connected to the actual mechanics

of a book. The air here
is a century long, which is not very long

for air. I still haven't checked *Meat Air* by Ron Loewinsohn
for that poem Jordan mentioned about the swimmers;

I should. I will. I fell off my horse and landed in the mud
on the side of the king's road to being a human person

and now you are looking at me, or feeling for me, it feels like
    pity
or it feels impossible, somehow, that you just continue

in your carriage on the dusty path into town that leads
eventually to the palace, Grace

Zabriskie giving you cryptic hints how to get there but not
the password you end up needing at the gate, the clue

you set up for yourself a lifetime ago was meant as a little
    joke, a knowing
nod, but you've forgotten the context and all you have

is an imm(ai)nent need to get to the other side, like someone
    dying
or a chicken in a different joke, one you get & could tell

was coming, a shipping crate full of joke books on fire
but the discard reason is listed as "water damage" anyway

& the nearby sea air is filled with the laughter of ashes
"swimming off to Catalina"

Bag of Water

That overstretched-rubber-band
-smell of old skunk, dead for days
on a part of the interstate sponsored
by the animal rehabilitation clinic

& wildlife rescue. When you buy
a bouquet they cannot give you
the vase it's sold in. They used to,
hence the FLOWERS ~~+ VASE~~ $12

sign, the strikethrough
& the plus looking like a sword
but instead of a stone it's
glass, always slowly flowing

even when all is going to plan
& nothing's broken except a ten
-year-old memory of your heart,
still surprisingly fresh ~~+ wet~~

Song

for Kristi

Wood is good
For a long time

Flowers,
Weeks

If you change
The water, cut off

The low greens so
They don't rot

In the vase.
The first time I saw

Your face was through a window,
A perihelion feeling

That revisits my bones
Every day. I only remember pieces

Of the prayer: *Thee by that exceeding pain,*
A meadow you hold open

Like a door

Tree of Life

> *One day, the sadness will end.*
> — Margaret Lanterman

On days when it's looking up
life insurance payout restrictions bad,

think of a little patch of bluebells
in the shade: it's dark, yes,

now, but the sun
is already beginning

its morning transit, will shift
the lattice of shadow

& light until those flowers,
too, see their moment of warm attention.

It will pass, yes,
that moment.

Do not mistake this
or be afraid. The stems'll shiver bluely again

in evening, for a brief time, but then the *moon*
will appear, its low glow giving

everything a dim & constant light

Espresso Powder

I say *are you serious* and my phone
googles the angry thing I meant
to say to the debt collector, who has me

on hold. I opened my heart to April
and became a serious liar, full
of dolls and music and more lateral

mistakes than I'm used to making,
five eggs in the from-scratch dough.
If you are invited to a party and do not know

the host, what do you bring? Not Jesus,
dripping with sirens. Not a lathe
even though you could offer to sharpen

every knife in the house.

Sheep in the Pyrenees

It's a fucks-given medley, arranged
by a jealous man with a terrible misprision
of who has done him wrong
and why. I will do the laundry tomorrow
and hear some of the same tunes
coming from the machine and
from my phone, scrolling through the cycles.

There is a heaviness to friends.

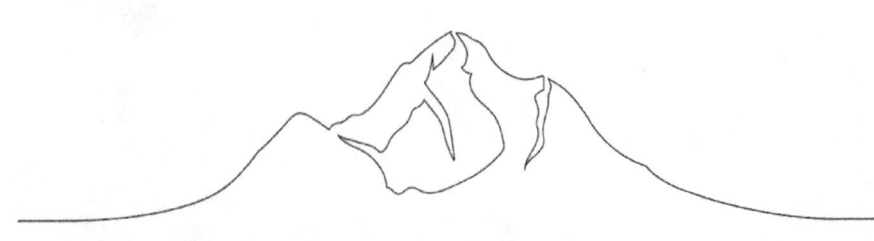

Keep Talking

Hounding for sapphires, my life
continues like a court case neither party
has their hearts in anymore. Legal fee days

give way to sluicewater nights, the river
is so cold you can't do
a whole pan in one go,

you have to split it up like gravel
in the crusher. My dreams
have gotten harder & harder

to remember, I know
I'm still having them somehow
but most mornings I awake blank, alarmed

& disprepared. Asparagus touches my head
gently, with a paw through the rods
holding up the stair rail.

Are you okay says his face.
Yes, you're okay says his walking away

Notes & Acknowledgments

"A Letter From The Mountain" first appeared on Metatron Press's *GLYPHÖRIA* platform. Part VII was written in 2014, using Google Translate to iteratively and lossily translate and retranslate the line "The theories think they've thought of everything." The translation started from English into the next language alphabetically on the platform (Esperanto), the output of which was then fed into the next language alphabetically and so on until the loop arrived back at just a single English word, "House."

*"Sonnet" should have an image, but the great bear of copyright has long claws. It first appeared at *Bullshit Lit* with the image intact, unafraid.

"Poem *(The trick is…)*" first appeared in *Frozen Sea*.

"Orange Rural Fire" and "Espresso Powder" first appeared in *Stone Circle Review*.

"Prose Poem" first appeared in *HAD*.

"Late Fee" and "OOAK" first appeared in *Rejection Letters*.

"Pan-American Strawberries" and "Metal, Pennsylvania" first appeared in *the tiny*.

"15 FLORÉAL" first appeared in *February 25*.

"Alcohol, Brutalism, Confetti" first appeared in *SWAMP*.

"William Butler Yeats" first appeared at *Back Patio*.

"Poem (*Money is…*)" first appeared in *berlin lit*.

"Song" first appeared in the *Neutral Spaces* magazine.

"Tree of Life" first appeared in *Poems for Tomorrow*.

"Keep Talking" first appeared at *ONLY POEMS*.

About the Author

Tom Snarsky is the author of the chapbooks *Threshold* (Another New Calligraphy) and *Complete Sentences* (Broken Sleep Books), as well as the full-length collections *Light-Up Swan* and *Reclaimed Water* (both from Ornithopter Press). His book *MOUNTEBANK* is forthcoming from Broken Sleep Books in 2026. He lives in the mountains of northwestern Virginia with his wife Kristi and their cats.

www.ingramcontent.com/pod-product-compliance
Lightning Source LLC
Chambersburg PA
CBHW062119080426
42734CB00012B/2918